Sports Strategies

BASEBALL STRATEGIES

BY DAVID J. CLARKE

SportsZone
An Imprint of Abdo Publishing
abdobooks.com

abdobooks.com

Published by Abdo Publishing, a division of ABDO, PO Box 398166, Minneapolis, Minnesota 55439.

Printed in the United States of America, North Mankato, Minnesota.
102023
012024

THIS BOOK CONTAINS RECYCLED MATERIALS

Cover Photo: Kyodo/AP Images
Interior Photos: Gregory Shamus/Getty Images Sport/Getty Images, 5; Al Bello/Getty Images Sport/Getty Images, 6–7; Rob Tringali/MLB Photos/Getty Images, 8; Sporting News/Getty Images, 11; Red Line Editorial, 13; John Adams/Icon Sportswire/Getty Images, 14–15; Ron Jenkins/Getty Images Sport/Getty Images, 16–17; Omar Rawlings/Getty Images Sport/Getty Images, 18; Harry How/Getty Images Sport/Getty Images, 21; Frank Franklin II/AP Images, 23; Joe Robbins/Icon Sportswire/Getty Images, 24–25; Matt Patterson/AP Images, 27; Nick Wosika/Icon Sportswire/AP Images, 28–29; Brian Blanco/Getty Images Sport/Getty Images, 31; Bettmann/Getty Images, 32; G Fiume/Getty Images Sport/Getty Images, 34–35; Alex Slitz/Getty Images Sport/Getty Images, 37; Focus on Sport/Getty Images, 39; Jed Jacobsohn/Getty Images Sport/Getty Images, 40–41; Vaughn Ridley/Getty Images Sport/Getty Images, 44–45

Editor: Steph Giedd
Series Designer: Joshua Olson

Library of Congress Control Number: 2023939418

Publisher's Cataloging-in-Publication Data

Names: Clarke, David J., author.
Title: Baseball strategies / by David J. Clarke
Description: Minneapolis, Minnesota: Abdo Publishing, 2024 | Series: Sports strategies | Includes online resources and index.
Identifiers: ISBN 9781098292423 (lib. bdg.) | ISBN 9798384910367 (ebook)
Subjects: LCSH: Sports teams--Juvenile literature. | Teamwork (Sports)--Juvenile literature. | Athletes--Training of--Juvenile literature. | Baseball--Juvenile literature.
Classification: DDC 796.01--dc23

TABLE OF CONTENTS

INTRODUCTION.................................4

CHAPTER 1
SHORTENING THE START........6

CHAPTER 2
LEADING WITH POWER.............16

CHAPTER 3
DEFENSIVE POSITIONING...........24

CHAPTER 4
SMALL BALL.....................................34

GLOSSARY 46
MORE INFORMATION 47
ONLINE RESOURCES 47
INDEX 48
ABOUT THE AUTHOR 48

INTRODUCTION

Baseball is a game of possibilities. Fans sit and watch upwards of three hours of game play. For most of that time, no action is happening. That empty time is filled with thinking about all the possible outcomes of the next pitch. How will the next moment play out? Everything that happens on the field is the result of a strategic decision. Some are made before the game or even the season, while others must be made in the heat of the moment.

A single baseball game is a fascinating collection of strategic moves. A pitcher and catcher must work together to outwit every hitter. Speedy base runners duel with opposing pitchers who have quick pickoff moves and catchers with rocket arms. Around the diamond, fielders try to get in perfect position before every pitch, hoping to turn a potential base hit into an out.

Team managers try to put together the best offensive lineup they can each game to attack the opposing team's pitcher. During the game, managers must think ahead, trying to anticipate any possible situation. Then they adjust to deal with whatever comes along during the game. Those small decisions can be the difference between winning and losing.

Baseball is a popular summer attraction.

Tigers
NAPA
DELTA
910AM
ADELL MEDIA
YANKEES
TIGERS
18
pepsi

CHAPTER 1

SHORTENING THE START

Cristian Javier was feeling it. The Houston Astros' starting pitcher opened Game 4 of the 2022 World Series with a three batters up, three batters out inning. No Philadelphia Phillies batters got a hit off the right-hander in the second inning either. He recorded his fourth strikeout of the game in the third. Then he struck out all three Phillies he faced in the fourth.

With each new inning, fans in Philadelphia got more and more on edge. Since the World Series was first held in

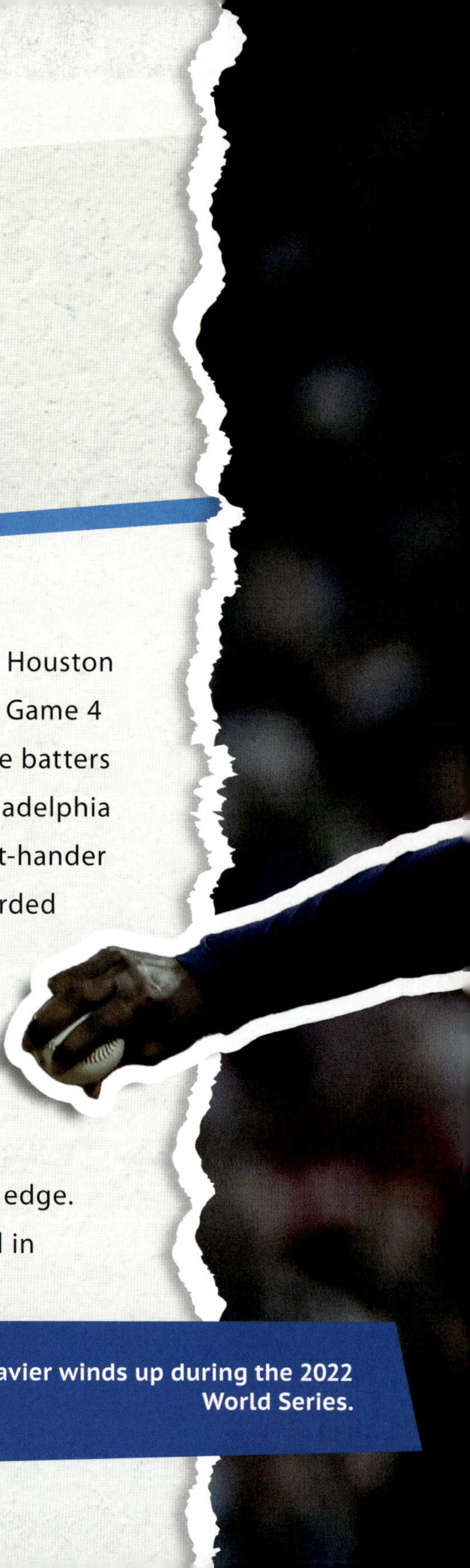

Houston Astros pitcher Cristian Javier winds up during the 2022 World Series.

WORLD SERIES
ROS
53

Astros manager Dusty Baker was also an MLB player. He played from 1968 to 1986, then became a manager in 1993.

1903, only one pitcher had recorded a no-hitter in a World Series game. That was Don Larsen of the New York Yankees, who threw a perfect game in the 1956 Fall Classic. Through six innings, Javier appeared to be on his way to becoming number two.

When the Astros jogged back onto the field for the bottom of the seventh, however, Javier was not with them. Instead, reliever Bryan Abreu trotted out to the pitcher's mound. Many fans watching the game could hardly believe it. Baseball traditionalists believed a pitcher throwing a no-hitter had the right to finish it off—or fail while trying. But Astros manager Dusty Baker had other ideas. He believed a fresh arm from the bullpen gave his team a better chance to win. Baker's decision eventually paid off. Houston ended up completing the no-hitter, with three relievers each pitching one inning in a 5–0 Astros win.

Baker's decision was controversial. Even after the Astros went on to win the World Series, fans were still debating whether he had made the right call. Baker proved one thing though. Baseball might be the most traditional of American sports, but when it comes to the bullpens, modern baseball managers do not hesitate to mix things up.

PULLING THE PITCHER

For much of baseball history, no player has been as important as the starting pitcher. This is the pitcher who begins the game. How he pitches sets the tone for the entire game. And in baseball's early years, he was simply *the* pitcher. If a pitcher started a game, then nine innings later he would end the game too. At the time, teams weren't even allowed to substitute a pitcher unless he became injured or ill.

That rule was changed in 1889, creating the concept of a bullpen. The bullpen is an area of the field where pitchers warm up before coming into a game. However, most people now use the term to refer collectively to the team's relief pitchers. These are the specialists who come in to replace the starting pitcher. Since 2021, a Major League Baseball (MLB) team is allowed to have 26 players on its roster at any given time. And as many as 13 of them can be pitchers. Typically five are starting pitchers, while seven or eight are relief pitchers. However, the makeup of bullpens, and how teams use them, has changed a lot over the years.

Originally, relievers were called on to pitch several innings, sometimes several times a week. Later, the idea of a top reliever to finish off victories evolved. These relievers were referred to as firemen at first, because they came into tough spots to "put out the fire." Later they became known as closers. During the 1980s, manager Tony La Russa introduced more new, specialized roles for his relievers. His closer only pitched the ninth inning if his team was ahead. The eighth inning belonged to his setup men. And the seventh inning was pitched

THE LOOGY

One of the more interesting bullpen roles in the 1990s and 2000s was that of a left-handed reliever who would come on in a key spot to try to get one left-handed hitter out. The Left-handed One Out Guy (LOOGY) became an important job in an MLB bullpen. However, the league changed its rules in 2020. After that, any pitcher who enters a game has to face at least three batters, unless the inning ends first. Overnight, the LOOGY ceased to exist.

Manager Tony La Russa, *second from left*, is in the Baseball Hall of Fame. He's earned three World Series titles and six pennants as a manager.

by a middle reliever. This basic philosophy became standard around baseball for several years. Typically teams aimed for the starting pitcher to handle the first six innings. Then, beginning in the seventh inning, relievers came in with fresh arms and pitches that the batters hadn't seen before.

This proved to be an effective approach. Starters faced less pressure to pitch late into games when their arms might be tiring. Meanwhile, teams started to develop specialized relievers who were able to execute specific jobs very well. All the while, starters still played a key role, often pitching late into the game.

SHORTENING THE GAMES

Even for teams with strong bullpens, starters still went the distance often. MLB pitchers tossed 290 complete games in 1996. But in the early 2000s, a data analysis revolution happened in the sport. One of the trends teams started to track was how starting pitchers became tired and suffered injuries from overuse.

Teams realized very quickly that pitchers were affected in two ways. By throwing too many innings, they were injuring themselves by repeating the same movements over and over. They were also much less effective once they passed 90 or 100 pitches. In addition, research showed that pitchers were less effective when facing a batter for the third time in a game. By then the hitter had seen the pitcher enough to be better prepared. As a result, managers began pulling pitchers much earlier. In 2021 the average start lasted just five innings. In 2022 MLB pitchers threw only 36 complete games.

Although data typically supports the decision to pull starting pitchers earlier, not everyone agrees. For much of baseball history, a pitcher's ability to last deep into a game was admired. The thinking was that, even if he didn't pitch a complete game, a pitcher who lasted longer allowed the bullpen to stay fresher. That made everybody better. In addition, rare pitching accomplishments such as a no-hitter or

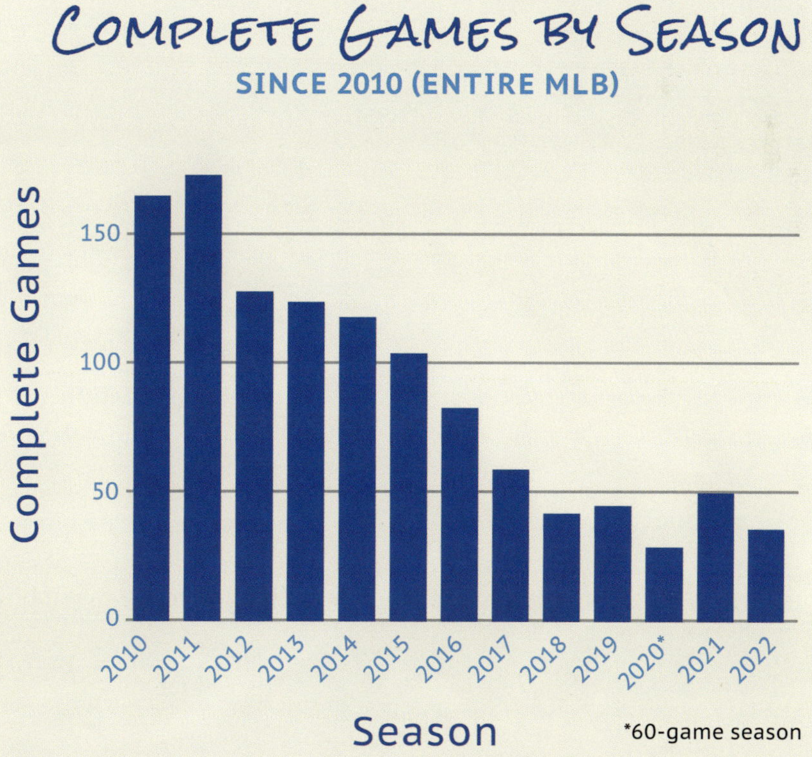

STROS
50

a perfect game were seen as historic feats. Witnessing one in person could be a lifelong memory for a fan.

For Baker and many others, however, the evidence has become too overwhelming. If a starting pitcher has been on the mound for too long, the manager doesn't hesitate to replace him. This showed earlier in the 2022 season when the Astros were facing the Yankees. Javier had struck out 13 of 23 batters through seven innings. But he had also thrown 115 pitches, so Baker pulled his starter. Relievers Hector Neris and Ryan Pressly each pitched an inning to complete the no-hitter. That same approach worked for the Astros in the postseason, when they went 11–2 with a 2.29 team earned-run average.

Astros reliever Hector Neris delivers a pitch in a 2023 game against the Atlanta Braves.

CHAPTER 2

LEADING WITH POWER

Aaron Judge was a towering figure as he stepped into the right-handed batter's box on October 4, 2022. At 6 feet, 7 inches tall and 282 pounds, Judge was one of the biggest players ever to play in the majors. And he had huge power to go along with his size.

It was the top of the first inning at Globe Life Field in Arlington, Texas. Judge was leading off the game as his New York Yankees were facing the Texas Rangers in the second game of a doubleheader. On the third pitch of his at-bat, Judge launched a

New York Yankees slugger Aaron Judge smiles as he rounds the bases after breaking Roger Maris's American League (AL) record for the most home runs in a season.

NEW YORK

Aaron Boone took over as the Yankees' manager in 2018.

home run to left field. As he rounded the bases, fans of both teams gave him a standing ovation. His teammates waited at home plate to congratulate the slugger. Judge had just hit his 62nd home run of the season. That broke the AL single-season record for home runs.

It was a great moment for baseball. But some longtime fans of the game, and even some former players, thought one part of Judge's accomplishment was strange. What was the best home-run hitter in baseball doing batting leadoff?

It was a question people had been asking for weeks. Judge had spent most of September and early October 2022 as the first hitter in the Yankees' batting order. The team's manager, Aaron Boone, had several reasons for the move. He said that even though his decision was not traditional, the game evolves and changes, as in other sports. If it helped the Yankees win, he was willing to be nontraditional.

PUZZLE PIECES

Throughout baseball history, one of a manager's most important jobs has been to put together a team's lineup. While most lineups stayed more or less the same, a manager might have made little changes. If a hitter was having a tough time, for example, the manager might move him lower in the batting order to take the pressure off. If a team was facing a left-handed pitcher, left-handed hitters might start the game on the bench.

A manager mixes and matches to give his team the best possible chance to win that day's game. However, for much of baseball history, every team was looking for the same thing out of the top spots in the order. The leadoff hitter got on base frequently and usually had good speed to steal bases. But he wasn't always the best hitter. The second spot was often a good contact hitter who could put the ball in play and

Schwarber Starts It Off

The Yankees weren't the only team to lead off with a power hitter during the 2022 season. The Philadelphia Phillies' Kyle Schwarber hit leadoff 123 times in 153 starts during the year. He led the National League (NL) with 46 home runs and helped the Phillies reach the World Series.

move the leadoff man along. Behind him was usually the hitter with the team's best batting average. The fourth spot was reserved for the top slugger.

The idea was to get the big bats to the plate with as many runners on base as possible. That way cleanup hitters, the fourth spot in the lineup, could have more chances for runs batted in. Most of the game's best power hitters throughout baseball history have hit either third or fourth. Barry Bonds set the MLB home-run record with 73 in 2001. He hit 66 of them from the third spot in the San Francisco Giants' batting order. When Judge was a rookie in 2017, he hit third more often than any other spot. That year he set a rookie record with 52 home runs.

EXTRA CHANCES

In 1987 MLB teams stole a league record 3,585 bases. Over the course of the next few decades, that number went down. In 2021 teams stole only 2,214 bases. And the league had four more teams in 2021 than it had 34 years earlier.

Barry Bonds looks on as his record-setting 73rd home run sails out of the stadium on October 7, 2001.

MLB teams began stealing fewer bases because managers decided it was too risky. It was determined that it was safer to get hitters on base and keep them moving with more walks and extra-base hits. And since leadoff hitters used to be chosen mainly for their speed, it didn't make sense to keep batting a weaker hitter at the top of the lineup.

The other thing teams realized when they started studying lineups was how much more often the top two spots get to bat. In 2019 a league study showed that leadoff and number two hitters bat about 50 more times per season than cleanup hitters. Managers jumped at the chance to get extra plate appearances for a player who could do serious damage with his bat, such as Judge.

EXTRA PROTECTION

Boone also made the move to give Judge better pitches to hit. Managers do their best to protect their best hitters. They do that by making sure that another dangerous hitter is batting right behind them. For most of the 2022 season, Judge hit in the second spot. First baseman Anthony Rizzo, who finished the year with 32 homers, hit third most games. While Rizzo wasn't as feared as Judge, he was good enough so that opposing pitchers couldn't just walk Judge and hope to get the next man out.

Judge moved to the leadoff spot in September when the regular leadoff man, DJ LeMahieu, was injured. Boone wanted to get Judge even more at-bats while the slugger chased the home-run record. But the move wasn't popular with everyone. After Judge struggled in the first two games of the AL Division Series (ALDS), analyst and former Yankee Alex Rodriguez said

Anthony Rizzo, *right*, celebrates a two-run homer hit by Aaron Judge, *left*, in a 2023 game.

hitting Judge leadoff was "gimmicky" baseball. However, Judge's numbers told a different story. In 34 games in the top spot during 2022, Judge hit .366 with an incredible .481 on-base percentage. He also hit 13 homers in those games.

Chapter 3

Defensive Positioning

The Kansas City Royals were in a tough spot on April 9, 2022. In the top of the 10th inning with the score tied 0–0, the visiting Cleveland Guardians had runners at first and third with only one out. Kansas City manager Mike Matheny decided to go to an old baseball strategy. He brought his infield in. The second baseman and shortstop both crept in several steps. They weren't all the way up on the grass. They didn't want to move in so far that they ruined their chance to turn a double play to end the inning. But first baseman Ryan O'Hearn and third

Bobby Witt Jr. of the Kansas City Royals makes a throw from third base during a game against the Cleveland Guardians on April 9, 2022.

KC
Royals
7

baseman Bobby Witt Jr. moved forward so that they were even with the two corner bases.

The next Cleveland hitter was Oscar Mercado. On a 1–2 pitch from Kansas City reliever Collin Snider, Mercado ripped a hard shot down the third-base line. Witt slid to his right to snare it with a backhand play. Without standing back up, Witt fired an off-balance throw home. Royals catcher Salvador Perez caught it on a hop, then tagged out Cleveland's Owen Miller for the second out.

Snider got the third out on the next batter. Kansas City won the game on a walk-off single in the bottom of the inning. But before they could win the game, the Royals had to keep Cleveland off the scoreboard. They did it by using one of baseball's oldest strategies.

COVERING THE SPACES

While offensive baseball has changed much in the 2000s, the basics of defensive baseball have stayed consistent throughout the sport's history. And while good pitching is the best way to play good defense, smart teams know how to position fielders correctly.

In the outfield, the three fielders can shift their position to anticipate where a batter will hit. For example, if a left-handed hitter normally hits into right field, the outfielders can line up

Fielders often position themselves based on where they think the batter will hit the ball.

more in that area. Outfielders can play deep near the wall to try to prevent extra-base hits from getting past them. Late in close games with a runner on third base, they can move up. There, they can catch shallow fly balls and be in a better position to make a throw to home plate to try to prevent the runner from scoring.

The infielders also have several positioning tactics they can use. Like outfielders, infielders will adjust their starting positions for certain hitters. Middle infielders might move closer to second base when there's a runner on first. That makes it easier to turn double plays quickly. With a runner on third base and fewer than two outs, teams often move the infield in, like the Royals did against the Guardians. That way the fielders are in a better position to protect home plate.

Defending bunt plays is an important part of infield defense. Frequently, fans will see the third baseman creeping up the baseline if he expects the hitter to bunt. The hope is that he can get the ball quickly and have time to throw the base runner out at second. One of the more exciting bunt defenses is the "wheel play." With runners on first and second, the first and third basemen charge toward home as soon as the pitcher starts

Depending on where the ball is hit, infielders know who should field a bunt. Many times, the catcher fields the ball since it's such a short hit.

Rawlings
RAWLINGS
RAWLINGS

his motion. At the same time, the shortstop sprints to cover third base. The second baseman sprints toward first. The center fielder crashes in to cover second base. The goal is to field the ball quickly and throw the lead runner out at third.

These defensive strategies are important because the nine defenders can't cover a baseball field. It's simply too big. Managers must decide where to take risks and leave some spaces open while covering others.

Sometimes that can lead to very strange setups. In Game 3 of the 2008 World Series, the Philadelphia Phillies had the bases loaded in the ninth inning. The Tampa Bay Rays brought one of their outfielders in and played with five infielders. The strategy didn't work, as the Phillies scored on a walk-off hit up the third-base line. But Tampa Bay manager Joe Maddon later defended the decision as worth the risk.

SHIFTING AND SHIFTING BACK

Maddon was known as the "mad scientist" when he managed the Rays. He was willing to try any setup in the field if he thought it would work. And he had data to back up his choices. By the mid-2000s, teams were using computer data to map out where on the field opposing hitters usually put the ball in play. Teams used that information to put defenders as close to the ball's normal landing spots as possible. Typically, that meant

Tampa Bay manager Joe Maddon looks over his lineup during a 2014 game against the Oakland Athletics.

shifting an extra infielder to the opposite side of second base. For left-handed hitters, the extra infielder would often line up in shallow right field. There were many cases of ground balls hit right at that fielder. Without the shift, the hits would be easy singles. Instead those batters were being thrown out at first base.

Boston Red Sox slugger Ted Williams is the all-time career leader in on-base percentage.

Shifts weren't a new idea. Teams had tried them as far back as the 1920s. The St. Louis Cardinals famously shut down legendary Boston Red Sox left-handed hitter Ted Williams in the 1946 World Series using a shift. However, as managers like Maddon saw better defensive results by shifting more often in the 2000s, every team started doing it, and seemingly all the time. Hitters had a hard time changing old batting habits. Teams got fewer hits when they put the ball in play, which led to less action during games.

Worried that the game was becoming less exciting for fans, MLB decided to make a rule change. The league restricted shifting starting in 2023. The new rules required defensive teams to line up two infielders on either side of second base on every hitter. And teams could no longer play with four players in the outfield. If any team broke those rules, the umpires would call an automatic ball until the players were moved back to the right spot. With those rules in place, teams again needed to rely on good fielders who could cover a lot of ground.

More New Rules

Banning shifting wasn't the only rule MLB put in place for 2023. The league also created a pitch clock to keep pitchers working quickly. They must start to deliver a pitch within 15 seconds with the bases empty or 20 seconds with runners on. The league also enlarged the bases and limited the number of times pitchers could attempt pickoff plays per at-bat. These two rules were designed to create more action by making it easier for players to steal bases.

Chapter 4

Small Ball

With each pitch, base runner Randy Arozarena of the Tampa Bay Rays kept moving farther and farther off third base. The Rays already led 4–0 over the Boston Red Sox in Game 1 of the 2021 ALDS. The momentum was on Tampa Bay's side. Arozarena was about to make sure it stayed that way.

The Red Sox had a shift on with a left-handed hitter at the plate. Boston's third baseman was playing well off the base, so Arozarena could afford to take a big lead.

During the 2022 season, Randy Arozarena ranked third in the AL in stolen bases, with 32.

RAYS

The Red Sox's pitcher was Josh Taylor. As a left-hander, he had his back to the runner on third.

Arozarena watched as four pitches were delivered to Rays hitter Brandon Lowe. As Taylor readied for the fifth delivery, he took his eye off Arozarena at third. The Tampa Bay runner was already halfway down the baseline, and then he took off sprinting. By the time Taylor realized what was happening and fired home, Arozarena was diving safely across the plate.

The Rays ended up winning the game 5–0. Though Boston rallied to win the series, Arozarena's gutsy play was a highlight of the 2021 playoffs. It was something he had wanted to try all year. "He asked me all season long, *verde, verde, verde*—'green light,'" said Tampa Bay manager Kevin Cash after the game. "We finally gave it to him."

DOING THE LITTLE THINGS

Arozarena's steal of home was a perfect example of "small ball." That term covers several baseball strategies designed to move a runner up a base. Stealing bases is one. Bunting is another. Some bunts are sacrifice bunts. Others can be squeeze bunts. On those plays, a bunter is trying to score a runner from third base. The squeeze bunt needs to be executed just right. Since the runner on third base often takes off when the pitch is thrown, a bunter who misses the ball is putting that runner

Ronald Acuña Jr. of the Atlanta Braves steals third base against the Los Angeles Dodgers during a 2023 game.

Heading for Home

Two innings before stealing home in Game 1 of the 2021 ALDS, Randy Arozarena hit a solo home run. He was the first player to do both in the same playoff game.

in a tough spot. The runner is often tagged or thrown out easily.

Another aspect of small ball is advancing runners with situational hitting. A common example is a sacrifice fly to score runs. Another example is a hitter intentionally grounding out to the right side of the infield with a runner on second base and no outs. That allows the runner to move to third base and gives the team a chance to get him in without a hit. Some ways that could happen would be with a passed ball or a wild pitch.

THE ART OF THE STEAL

Like good fielding, playing small ball has been a fundamental part of baseball throughout the sport's history. In MLB's early days, home runs were rare. The early 1900s were known as the "dead ball era." Teams had to create runs with singles, bunts, and stolen bases. Even as home runs became a big part of the game in the 1920s and beyond, most teams still used small-ball techniques often, especially when the team's weaker hitters were up to bat.

Hall of Famer Rickey Henderson, *left*, was a nightmare for pitchers due to his speed and instincts on the base paths.

Stolen bases have always been one of the most exciting parts of baseball. Players who could get on base and cause havoc for opposing pitchers thrilled fans. No one was better than Rickey Henderson. He set a record for stolen bases with

1,406 between 1979 and 2003. Opponents were terrified to let Henderson get on base. Former teammate Mitchell Page said having Henderson on your team was like starting every game ahead 1–0.

One of the most famous stolen bases in MLB history came in the 2004 AL Championship Series (ALCS). The Boston Red Sox were losing the series to the New York Yankees 3–0. New York then built a one-run lead in the bottom of the ninth inning of Game 4 at Boston's Fenway Park. With no outs, Boston pinch runner Dave Roberts came into the game after teammate Kevin Millar walked. Everyone in the ballpark knew the speedy Roberts would try to steal second at some point. He still pulled it off, just barely beating Yankee catcher Jorge Posada's throw to second base. Roberts then scored on a base hit and tied the game. Boston won in extra innings, kicking off a historic comeback. The Red Sox also won the next three games

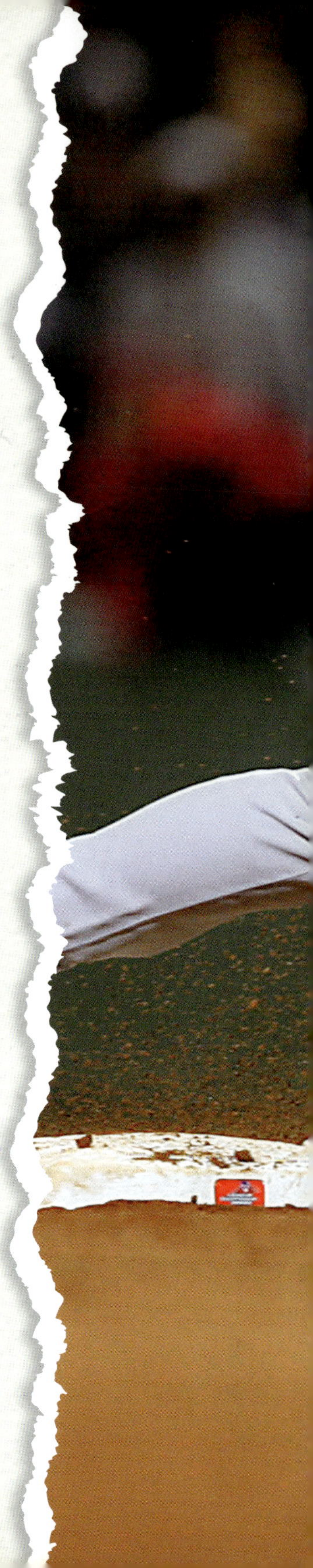

Dave Roberts steals second base safely, beating Derek Jeter's tag during the 2004 ALCS.

to take that series, becoming the first MLB team ever to come back from being down 3–0 in a best-of-seven series. They then swept the St. Louis Cardinals in the World Series for the Red Sox's first championship in 86 years.

DISAPPEARING SMALL BALL

Many teams that have analyzed hitting in the 2000s have turned away from small-ball tactics. Teams don't like the idea of trading outs for runs or to move runners up. Others have decided that stealing bases is just too risky. They believe that it's better to save the outs and try to get runners home by extra-base hits and home runs.

Several teams took those ideas to the extreme in 2022. Ten teams recorded fewer than 10 sacrifice bunts all year. One, the Atlanta Braves, hadn't logged a sacrifice until the second-to-last day of the regular season. Atlanta was second in the majors with 243 home runs. That strategy clearly worked for the Braves, who won 101 games.

KEEP THE LINE MOVING

Most championship teams in the 2010s and 2020s have been power-hitting clubs. One big exception was the 2015 Kansas City Royals. That season Kansas City hit only 139 homers, one of the lowest totals in the league. The Royals didn't bunt much either, but their 104 stolen bases ranked among the most in the league.

Another thing the Royals did well that year was to put the ball into play. As teams have swung for the fences, strikeout totals in MLB have exploded. In 2015 each of the other 29 MLB teams struck out more than 1,100 times. The Royals' total was just 973. By simply putting the ball in play more often, Kansas City was tough to beat. The team's slogan became "Keep the Line Moving." The Royals rode that slogan all the way to the team's first World Series title in 30 years.

One of the Royals' biggest playoff moments that year came in Game 4 of the ALDS against the Houston Astros. Kansas City entered the top of the eighth inning trailing 6–2. A loss would have meant the end of the season for the Royals, who trailed 2–1 in a best-of-five series. But Kansas City started the eighth with five straight singles. A Houston error followed by a stolen base and two walks added to the rally.

KINGS OF SMALL BALL

The kings of small ball might have been the 1982 St. Louis Cardinals. That year, St. Louis hit a league low 67 home runs. But St. Louis made up for it by stealing 200 bases. In the World Series, St. Louis topped the slugging Milwaukee Brewers, who had led MLB with 216 homers, in seven games to win the title.

6

When it was all over, the Royals led 7–6 on their way to a 9–6 win. It was proof that even in a power-hitting era, the little things could win big games.

Royals base runner Lorenzo Cain, *left*, slides safely into home during the 2015 ALCS against the Toronto Blue Jays.

GLOSSARY

cleanup
The fourth hitter in the team's lineup and typically the most powerful.

closer
A pitcher who comes in at the end of the game to secure a win for his team.

error
A mistake in the field made by a baseball player.

fundamental
Basic or important.

leadoff
The first hitter in a team's lineup.

no-hitter
A complete game in which a team does not allow any hits.

perfect game
A complete game in which a team retires every opposing batter and allows no base runners.

postseason
The playoffs, including the wild-card round, divisional playoffs, league championship series, and World Series.

rally
A series of walks and hits that result in multiple runs.

revolution
A significant change.

sacrifice fly
A fly ball that a fielder catches for an out, but that results in a base runner scoring.

walk-off
A victory in which the home team scores the winning run in the bottom of the final inning.

MORE INFORMATION

Books

Clarke, David J. *Kansas City Royals.* Minneapolis, MN: Abdo Publishing, 2023.

Hewson, Anthony K. *GOATs of Baseball.* Minneapolis, MN: Abdo Publishing, 2022.

Hewson, Anthony K. *Houston Astros.* Minneapolis, MN: Abdo Publishing, 2023.

Online Resources

Booklinks
NONFICTION NETWORK
FREE! ONLINE NONFICTION RESOURCES

To learn more about baseball strategies, please visit **abdobooklinks.com** or scan this QR code. These links are routinely monitored and updated to provide the most current information available.

INDEX

Abreu, Bryan, 8
Arozarena, Randy, 34–36, 38
Atlanta Braves, 42

Baker, Dusty, 8–9, 15
Bonds, Barry, 20
Boone, Aaron, 19, 22
Boston Red Sox, 32, 34–36, 40–42

Cash, Kevin, 36
Cleveland Guardians, 24–26, 28

Fenway Park, 40

Globe Life Field, 16

Henderson, Rickey, 39–40
Houston Astros, 6, 8–9, 15, 43

Javier, Cristian, 6–8, 15
Judge, Aaron, 16–20, 22–23

Kansas City Royals, 24–26, 28, 42–43

La Russa, Tony, 10
Larsen, Don, 8
LeMahieu, DJ, 22
Lowe, Brandon, 36

Maddon, Joe, 30, 32
Matheny, Mike, 24
Mercado, Oscar, 26
Millar, Kevin, 40
Miller, Owen, 26

Neris, Hector, 15
New York Yankees, 8, 15, 16, 19, 20, 22–23, 40

O'Hearn, Ryan, 24

Page, Mitchell, 40
Perez, Salvador, 26
Philadelphia Phillies, 6, 20, 30
Posada, Jorge, 40
Pressly, Ryan, 15

Rizzo, Anthony, 22
Roberts, Dave, 40
Rodriguez, Alex, 22

San Francisco Giants, 20
Schwarber, Kyle, 20
Snider, Collin, 26
St. Louis Cardinals, 32, 42, 43

Tampa Bay Rays, 30, 34–36
Taylor, Josh, 36
Texas Rangers, 16

Williams, Ted, 32
Witt, Bobby, Jr., 24–26

About the Author

David J. Clarke is a freelance sportswriter. Originally from Helena, Montana, he now lives in Savannah, Georgia, with his golden retriever, Gus.